The New C

Finding God when we meet together

Member's Coursebook

edited by Roger Morgan

The New Community is Book 2 of *The God Who Is There*, the ReSource discipleship course for small groups

ReSource

Copyright © Roger Morgan 2012
The right of Roger Morgan to be identified as the author of this work has been asserted by him in accordance with the Copyright, Designs and Patents Act 1988.

All rights reserved. No part of this publication may be reproduced, stored in a retrieval system, or transmitted in any form or by any means, electronic, mechanical, photocopying, recording or otherwise, without the prior written permission of the copyright owner.

Published by:
ReSource
13 Sadler Street, Wells, Somerset BA5 2RR
office@resource-arm.net
www.resource-arm.net
Charity no. 327035

ISBN 978-1-906363-33-8

Unless otherwise stated, all Bible translations are taken from the New Revised Standard Version of the Bible, Anglicized edition, copyright © 1989, 1995 by the Division of Christian Education of the National Council of the Churches of Christ in the United States of America, and are used by permission. All rights reserved.

Cover photo © istockphoto.com
Images on pp 95,17,20,28,38,48,54,57,60 © iStockphoto.com
Images on pp 7,8,18,22,23,25,28,35,40,42,45,47,49,50,51 © Fotolia.co.uk
Images on pp 13,14,15,18a,32,38,42 © Microsoft.com
Images on pp 10,24,37 © Alison Morgan
Image on p 55 © Martin Cavender
Images on pp 29,31 Public Domain

This course is edited by Roger Morgan, working with Anita Benson and Alison Morgan. The following people contributed to the writing of the individual sessions: John Benson, Ian Bishop, Pete Greaves, Mike Harrison, Richard Morgan, Michael Selman, Karin Silk, Elaine Sutherland, Lauren Wicks, Angela Zvespar.

The New Community

Contents

Preface	Page 4
1. Baptism – joining the community	Page 5
2. Honouring the holy presence of God	Page 11
3. Praise	Page 16
4. Looking back and looking forward	Page 21
5. Learning to pray together	Page 27
6. More about prayer	Page 33
7. Expressing our love for God	Page 39
8. The power of words	Page 46
9. A community of love	Page 52
10. Deepening our love	Page 58
Song words	Page 65

Preface

Welcome to the three-part ReSource series on discipleship, *The God Who Is There*. The first book, *Beyond Ourselves,* begins with the simple question 'Is God really there?', and then helps people find a living faith in him. This second book, *The New Community,* is about finding God to be there whenever a group of Christians come together. The third book, *Shining Like Stars*, is about finding God to be there in ordinary day-to-day life.

The God Who Is There takes its inspiration from an earlier series, *Rooted in Jesus*, written in 2002 for rural Africa and now in use in 28 languages and 14 countries. Because of its success in Africa many people asked us to release *Rooted in Jesus* for use in the West, and *The God Who Is There* is our response; it has the same aims and conversational style as *Rooted in Jesus*, and much overlapping content. At first we thought we could keep the same structure and session titles, but we found that the cultural differences between Africa and the West meant that in practice we needed to rewrite the course completely – particularly in this second book, which we think is radically different from anything you will find elsewhere. In *Beyond Ourselves* the challenge was to relate the material to western moral and philosophical assumptions. In *The New Community* the challenge has been to present the corporate nature of discipleship and the essence of worship in the context of our individualistic, consumer-driven society.

Taken together the three books in this series are our attempt to explain the fundamentals of Christian discipleship. In the first book we learned that discipleship is entering into a relationship with God, a relationship based on promises and therefore on faithfulness and trust. In this second book we learn that discipleship is not just an individual thing; discipleship is intended as a group activity, a shared journey in which we find a new identity as part of a community centred on Jesus. Finally, in the third book we learn that discipleship is about how we conduct our lives in the daily reality of our families and communities. In all the ups and downs of everyday life we find that God is there setting us standards, leading us on, and helping us at every turn.

The New Community

Session 1: Baptism – joining the community

Summary of the session

> The first Christian community or church was formed in Jerusalem on the day of Pentecost. First these people heard a message about Jesus; then they repented of their sins, were baptised and received the Holy Spirit. Today, whenever a group of people take these same steps, the Holy Spirit will come to them in the same way, and form them into a new community in which God is present. This community can be likened to a body in which we are the members and Jesus is the head.
>
> Baptism is the outward action or ceremony by which people join the new community and receive the Spirit. Baptism pictures the end of the old life and the beginning of the new. It pre-figures for us the day when our bodies will die and then be raised to new life. Baptism is essential for every Christian; it is by baptism that we identify with Jesus.
>
> Jesus experienced the Holy Spirit powerfully at his baptism. It will probably be the same for us. For some, though, the gift of the Spirit comes first and is then followed by baptism.
>
> Should the children of believers be baptised? This issue has long divided Christians and it is best that we respect each other's practices.

Key verse

1 Corinthians 12.13 – 'For in the one Spirit we were all baptised into one body – Jews or Greeks, slaves or free – and we were all made to drink of one Spirit.'

Exercises following Session 1

Please complete one of these four exercises before you come to the next session; choose whichever one seems best for you. If you have time you may wish to complete more than one. The first three are aimed at helping you to explore what you learned in the first session. The fourth is a preparation for the next session.

Exercise 1 – Scripture memory

This exercise is for those groups who have decided to commit the key verses to memory. If you are going to learn the verses it will help you to have a system. So let's suppose that this week's key verse, **1 Corinthians 12.13,** is your first ever memory verse.

1. Every day check that you can say **1 Corinthians 12.13** by heart. Do this at the end of the day, making sure that you are word perfect before you go to sleep. Word perfect means being able to recite the reference as well as the verse.

2. The next morning check that you can still say both reference and verse correctly.

3. If the verses you learn are to change your life then you must add meditation to the memorisation. During the day, whenever you can, meditate on **1 Corinthians 12.13**. Don't plan special meditation times. Just use all those times when your mind is free – for example when you are waiting for someone, or walking alone for a few minutes. Meditate by thinking carefully and prayerfully about the verse, one word at a time. Continue with the meditation next time your mind is free.

4. Whenever you have the chance, share your thoughts about **1 Corinthians 12.13** with someone else.

5. After a week of living with **1 Corinthians 12.13** you will find that you are word perfect. It will then be time to take on a new verse. Perhaps you will choose to learn **Matthew 18.20**, the key verse for the next session. Do the same with the new verse as you did with the first one, but keep the first one going as well. Each day before you go to sleep make sure you are word perfect for both verses. In the morning check up on both. During the day meditate on both. And whenever you can, share your thoughts on either of the verses with someone else.

6. In the third week add a third verse and so on. After six weeks you will have six verses on the go. In the seventh week add a new verse but also drop the first one. If you keep on going like this you will always be meditating on six verses every day, but the ones you have dropped will never be forgotten from your memory and never lose their influence on your life and your ministry to others.

Exercise 2 – Decisions about baptism

This exercise is about taking up the various challenges that arise from the teaching about baptism which you received in the session.

1. The first challenge is for anyone who has become a Christian but has not yet been baptised. An unbaptised Christian is still a Christian, a child of God, a member of God's family. But even so to be a Christian and remain unbaptised is like being in love with someone and living with them, but never going through with the marriage ceremony. Jesus wants all those who become his disciples to take part in the baptism ceremony and make their vows to him in public. If you are up to this challenge, give your group leader a ring and ask him/her to arrange for you to be baptised. And invite all your friends along to watch, believers and non-believers alike.

2. This challenge is for someone who was baptised long ago, perhaps as a baby. At the time you did not really make a full commitment to Christ and you did not experience a relationship with him. But now that you have become a Christian in the fullest sense you may be asking 'should I be baptised again?' For you there are various possible ways forward and different church leaders will give you different advice. Some will advise you to be baptised again, but this time by full immersion. Others will advise you to be confirmed. Others will say that you do not need to do anything. Still others will want to leave the decision to you. In the end it is up to you. Have a chat with your group leader or church leader and then decide what to do. Try to do what you think Jesus would want you to do.

3. This challenge is for parents of young children who have not been part of a church up to now. Now that you have become a Christian, God regards

your children as part of his family just as you are and so, if your partner agrees, it is wise to start bringing them to church. They are unlikely to protest; they will have a fun time and learn a lot. Once the children are part of the church it is best that they too formally join the church. In some churches the practice is to baptise children. In other churches there is a different kind of joining ceremony. Unless the children are tiny the meaning of the ceremony should be explained very carefully to them, and it certainly should not happen against their will.

4. The final challenge is the most important of all. Joining the new community is far more than merely taking part in a formal ceremony. When you join the new community you commit yourself to those specific people to be with them, to love them, to pray for them, and to worship God with them. In our culture many people are reluctant to commit to communities of any kind; this is happening in the secular world as well as in the church. So look carefully at **Hebrews 10.25**; if it is at all possible, make up your mind to re-organise your life so that you can always be there when your group meets. Let your group leader know that you have understood that being a Christian means being a part of a community of Christians and that, until God directs otherwise, you would like to be a committed and wholehearted member of your group.

Exercise 3 – Reliving your baptism

This exercise is an act of personal devotion which should take about half an hour. It is a way of re-living your baptism. It can be done on your own or with a friend. The exercise will work well without music, but if you have a personal copy of the course CD then use it. Listen to the suggested songs and, if you know the words, sing them.

Begin by looking at **Ephesians 2.1-3**. Notice that before you became a Christian and were baptised the following things were true of you.

- You were spiritually dead
- Your values were more or less the same as the world's values
- Satan had a great influence on how you lived

- You were affected by the need to meet the desires of your body
- You were affected by the need to meet the desires of your mind
- You were subject to the anger of God and therefore in grave danger of judgment and punishment

Think carefully about each one of these. Do you agree that there was a time when you were like this?

Now that you have become a Christian and been baptised, all these things belong to your past and not to the present. To help you picture this, lie on the floor face up with your eyes closed and your hands at your sides as if you were lying in a coffin. As you lie there reflect that the old you is dead, gone, buried. And, if you have the music available, listen to track 14, 'Jesus I have forgotten'.

Stay down there for a few minutes and then stand upright with your eyes open and your hands raised. The dead person is now alive. Thank God for your new life. Ask him once again to receive you as his child and fill you with his Spirit. If the music is available play track 18 'Jesus, all for Jesus'. As you stand listen to the music and join in the song.

Now look at **Ephesians 2.4-10**, which describes your life after baptism. Every one of the things listed above has changed. Thank God for each one:

- Thank God that there is now clear evidence that you are spiritually alive
- Thank God that your values have begun to change
- Thank God that in your life his voice has begun to drown out Satan's voice
- Thank God that you are learning to say 'no' to the demands of your body
- Thank God that you are learning to say 'no' to the demands of your mind
- Thank God that you are no longer subject to his anger but have become his child, subject only to his loving discipline

Putting it more positively, you are learning the joys of committing yourself to God's ways so that the old ways no longer seem so attractive.

There are two underlying themes to the changes that are coming about in your life. First of all you are learning to receive – God has an endless supply of good things for you, and you are beginning to realise this and benefit from it. And secondly you are learning to submit. The Christian life begins with submission to baptism and continues as we submit to the changes which God wants to bring about in our lives.

Stand again and lift up your arms again to heaven. Spend a few moments receiving God's blessings. Then kneel and bow your head. Submit to his will and wait for his instructions. If music is available play track 6 'I'm giving you my heart'. If you know the words sing them.

Exercise in preparation for Session 2

Think about the group to which you belong, and its huge potential. Start by looking at **1 Peter 2.1-10.** Your group is like a building in which each of the members are stones and Jesus is the cornerstone. Think about what will happen to a building if some of the stones are removed. Pray for each member of your group that they will stand firm in their membership of the building to which you now all belong.

Turn next to **1 Corinthians 3.16** which identifies this building as being rather like the ancient Jewish temple which had been built on a hill in Jerusalem. This temple was always thought of as a special place where God could live on earth. Now you, the church, are that temple. Together you are that special place where God lives.

Turn to **Ezekiel 47** and read verses 1-12. In Ezekiel's vision a river flows out of the temple. Reflect that a river is going to flow out of your group. Look at **John 7.38** where Jesus too says that this is what will happen. Now close your eyes and hold this picture in your mind. God's blessing is going to flow from your group like a stream of water and there will be more and more of it, and more and more fish, and more and more fruit. Ask God to make this the shared vision of all in your group.

The New Community

Session 2: Honouring the holy presence of God

Summary of the session

> Any group of Christians who regularly meet together in the name of Jesus constitute a church, though they may also be part of a larger church. When the group (church) meets Jesus promises that he will always meet with us. If Jesus is present then the Father is present and the Holy Spirit is also present. They are not just present in theory – they are really present. We should expect them to reveal themselves to us whenever we meet.
>
> When we meet together we acknowledge the presence of God and honour him. Because God is so great and so holy the only natural way to honour him is to worship him. One way of worshipping God is to bow down before him. As our hearts and our wills bow down in reverence before God it is good to reflect this both by our posture and by the way that we sing.
>
> This respect for God which Christians express when they meet together is to be then taken out by each Christian into daily life. All day every day we bow before God by striving to please him in the way that we live our lives. God is perfect so we too will aim for perfection.

Key verse

Matthew 18.20 – 'For where two or three are gathered in my name, I am there among them.'

Exercises following Session 2

Please complete at least one of these four exercises before you come to the next session; choose whichever one seems best for you. The first three will help you to explore what you learned in this session. The fourth is a preparation for the next session.

Exercise 1– Aiming for perfection

Turn to Matthew's gospel chapters 5-7. This is some teaching by Jesus usually referred to as 'The Sermon on the Mount'. Jesus outlines the standards by which he himself lived and by which he wants his disciples to try to live. If you have time, read the whole passage and realise that Jesus' standards are very high. Jesus is inviting us, his disciples, to seek after perfection. Turn to **Matthew 5.48** and you will see why. We seek perfection because our God himself is perfect. Our God is a holy God which means that he is set apart, or that he is different from us. By striving after perfection, we are trying to set ourselves apart too, to be like God. This is our way of honouring God and telling him we love him.

Here are some of the principles which Jesus taught in this sermon. Choose one which you know you are not going to find easy, and try hard to live by it this week. If you want to be really ambitious, and God stirs your heart, go for more than one.

- **Chapter 5.21-22**: Aim for the ideal of always keeping your tongue under control. Don't shout at anyone, insult anyone, call anyone names. Instead stay calm even if you are severely provoked. If you are provoked and feel your anger boiling up, turn immediately to prayer and ask God to help you find self-control.

- **Chapter 5.23-24**: Think of someone with whom you have a bad relationship. Jesus calls us to the ideal of seeking to be at peace with everyone. It does take two to make peace, but the challenge is to do whatever you can. So go and see this person and try to sort things out.

- **Chapter 5.27-29**: The opposite sex is all around us and we are bound to notice. Sexual images are everywhere. But this week when you notice these things turn your eyes and your thoughts away and think about something else. God wishes most of us to have one person, someone we love and who loves us, and with whom we can enjoy the pleasure of sexual union. God calls us to the ideal of lifelong faithfulness to this person even in our thought life. Some people are called to be single as Jesus was, but if you are single and struggling with it, then ask God to provide what you so obviously seem to need. Ask others to pray for you too.

- **Chapter 5.37**: In this verse Jesus sets us the ideal of being faithful to our word. If we promise to do something we will do it no matter how inconvenient it may turn out to be. If we make an appointment we will be there and on time. If we owe someone money we will pay them and on time.

- **Chapter 6.6**: Take twenty minutes every day to find a lonely place and pray – but don't tell anyone what you are doing. There are times when it is good to meet to pray with others, but we also need times of private prayer.

- **Chapter 6.12**: Each day before you go to bed think about the things that you have done wrong today. Confess these to God and receive his forgiveness. Also think about who has behaved badly towards you today. Ask your Father to forgive them and not hold what they have done against them.

- **Chapter 6.33-34**: It may be good to plan ahead, but we should never worry ahead! So this week, whenever you find yourself worrying about the things that lie ahead, discipline yourself to switch your mind onto other things. If there is a problem about what to do or say at some point in the future, do not think about it today but leave it until you have to think about it. When the time comes God will show you the way.

Exercise 2 – Photographs

Take or ask for photographs of each member of the group. Put them on your phone or computer, or make a collage and put them up on the wall. From time to time look at the pictures and pray for each person. These people are now your family. Pray that they will be a good family.

Lift each one to God, and ask him to give you a vision for that person – something that is going to happen in their life or some way in which they are going to change.

You will find that for some members of the group this vision will be immediately clear. Don't say anything; just keep on praying until something happens. In some cases you will find yourself praying for something that seems almost impossible, but do not worry because God is the God of the seemingly impossible! Just keep on praying.

For other members of the group, clarity of vision will be much harder to find. In your prayers return again and again to that person. Think carefully about them, lift them up before God, and keep asking how you should pray for them.

Exercise 3 – Removing your shoes

Begin this exercise in a quiet place in a room where you cannot be disturbed, or a quiet spot in the open air. Then read **Exodus 3.1-6**.

You will see that Moses suddenly became aware of the presence of God, and he removed his shoes as a mark of respect. You do the same – become aware of the presence of God, and remove your shoes. Then stand with your head bowed and pray. Stay like this for a while.

Now lift your arms up high in praise to God and sing as you sang in the group 'He is Lord, he is Lord, he has risen from the dead and he is Lord' (Track 5 on the CD). Sing to him with all your heart. No one else can hear you, but God definitely can.

Then kneel in his presence and be very quiet. Become aware of how small you are and how big he is. Become aware of how weak you are and how strong he is. Become aware of how sinful you are and how holy he is. Confess your sins to God and receive his peace.

Finally lie flat on the floor, face down, before God. This is a posture of total surrender. Stay like this for a few minutes. Then read what God said to Moses in **Exodus 3.7-10**. What is God saying to you? Ask him to speak.

Later in the day, or perhaps later in the week, find a church or chapel where you can be alone for a few minutes. Read **Isaiah 6.1-8.** For a little while become Isaiah sitting in the temple; experience what he experienced. Then stand up and approach the altar. Stand facing the altar with your head bowed. If the church has no altar, find a cross and stand before the cross. Then lift your hands to heaven and sing as loudly as you dare, 'He is Lord, he is Lord, he is risen from the dead and he is Lord'. Then lie face down and surrender yourself to him.

Exercise in preparation for Session 3

This exercise is aimed at getting a glimpse of just how big the mind of God is. It takes about an hour, and can be done alone or with one or two others.

Go for a walk from your house to the nearest library or bookshop and take a notebook with you. On the way, look around you, observe every living thing that crosses your path, and make a note in your notebook. Notice trees, flowers, birds, insects, animals. Write down the names of every species you know and a description of the ones you don't know. When you get to the bookshop or library make a note of all the subjects that have been written about by the authors of the books. Time will be short so you will inevitably have to limit the length of time you take making this list.

As you walk home look up and imagine. We know that beyond everything that we can see, beyond even the sun itself, there is galaxy after galaxy after galaxy. Almost everything exists is completely out of your sight, and always will be. When you get home reflect on what you have been doing. You have been seeing and touching an infinitesimally small part of God's mind. Now look with gratitude at **John 1.18**.

The New Community

Session 3: Praise

Summary of the session

> Praise is expressing to someone else how much we like or admire them for who they are or what they have done.
>
> Praise is a wholesome activity in all relationships, and we should cultivate the habit of praising others whenever we can do so sincerely. Praise is also an essential part of our relationship with God.
>
> If things are going wrong in our lives it is harder to praise God, but if we do choose to praise him then God will reward us for our faith.
>
> Praising is a way into God's presence; as we choose to praise God then we will find that God reveals himself to us. As we become aware of his presence with us, then it will be natural for us to worship him. So praise leads easily into worship.
>
> Christians who have been in the presence of a holy God find that the unholy desires which are found in every human heart are burned away by his presence. So praise leads naturally to holiness.

Key verse

1 Peter 1.14-15 – 'Like obedient children, do not be conformed to the desires that you formerly had in ignorance. Instead, as he who called you is holy, be holy yourselves in all your conduct.'

Exercises following Session 3

Please complete at least one of these four exercises before you come to the next session; choose whichever one seems best for you.

Exercise 1 – Praising other people

Praise is telling another person what you like about them. Praising other people is good – both for the one being praised and for the one doing the praising. If a person has twenty bad points and one good one, it is not insincere to praise the good point, and we normally do very little good by mentioning the twenty.

So aim in this next week to see how many people you can sincerely praise, and observe the effect your praises have on them. In particular go out of your way to praise the people you live and work with.

The simplest form of praise is thanks. For example, at home someone makes a meal for us and we thank them. Or we buy something in a shop or in a restaurant, and we thank the person who has served us.

Sometimes praise and thanks are expressed well by sending a card. Who are the helpful people in your life? Is it time to send them a card to thank them for who they are and what they mean to you? Sometimes it is good to go further than a card and send a small gift.

It is good to praise a kind action, whether one offered to you or one offered to someone else. It is good to praise achievement by offering congratulations. It is good to praise someone who has died, perhaps in a letter to the bereaved.

Personal remarks can be risky even when sincere. It is not always wise for a man to say to someone else's wife 'I think you are very beautiful'. But personal remarks do often cheer people. 'I like your dress,' or 'I love your smile,' or 'I admire your courage' are the kind of remarks that lift another person.

Within the family, and also in the family of the church, praise should be endless. Praise is hugely important in every successful marriage, and vital in helping children to grow up believing in themselves.

So this week make a habit of handing out praise at every opportunity.

Exercise 2 – Praising God by singing

The best way to praise God on a daily basis is to sing. If you sing a lot you will find both that you become a happier person, and that you feel closer and closer to God. So sing as you go.

This week, try and build singing into your life. You will need an MP3 player or iPod, or a CD player – perhaps you have one in your car. Get hold of some music which you can sing along to. An obvious choice would be to order a copy of the course CD, and plan to become familiar with all of the songs.

Exercise 3 – Cutting out the bad stuff

In this exercise we continue the search for personal holiness. **Galatians 5.19-21** gives a list of bad things which are sometimes found in the lives of Christians. Look at **Matthew 5.29-30** where Jesus is teaching that determined steps are needed if we are to get rid of these things. Here are some of the things Paul lists for the Galatians:

- **Fornication.** Many people have sex with someone they are not married to (this is what the word fornication refers to). For Christians this is not acceptable. But it is not easy to give up, and if this is a problem for you, you will probably need others to pray for you as you try to make the change. Once this area of your life is under control you will be so pleased and feel so free.

- **Idolatry**. When we worship a god who is not the same as the God of the Bible, or seek power and guidance from a different god from the God of Jesus, then we are guilty of idolatry. The most common examples of idolatry are spiritualism, freemasonry, and all forms of 'occult' practice. If you have been involved in any of these things you may find that it is hard to give them up. Why, you will say, can't I be both a Freemason and a Christian? The problem is that any form of idolatry is a way of giving Satan power in your life, and he will use this power to harm you and your family. So find someone to talk to who you can trust, and look forward to the freedom you will experience when you close the doorway to Satan.

- **Quarrels**. Many people are involved in quarrels or bitter arguments, often with family members, sometimes with neighbours. But the Bible tells us to live at peace with everyone so far as it depends on us. And Jesus taught his disciples to resolve every argument as quickly as possible. So if there is anyone with whom you have a feud or an ongoing conflict, take steps to end it. Go to them, apologise for your part, and ask if you can be friends.

- **Drunkenness**. Many people drink too much and some are addicted to drink. Others use other kinds of drugs. These habits are very hard to shift, but with prayer and determination and the help of friends it can be done. There are many former alcoholics to be found in our churches – people who are praising God every day for their freedom.

Exercise in preparation for Session 4

From the earliest times Christians have always shared bread and wine when they meet together. All Christian groups do this, and so will you in the next session. To understand the origins of this practice read

Matthew 26.17-30. Taking bread and wine together is a symbolic action.

At most wedding services bride and groom give each other a ring. This too is a symbolic action. The rings are given as a promise of endless love and faithfulness. The shape of the ring symbolises this because the ring goes on and on, never coming to an end. The ceremony of baptism is also full of symbols. When the candidate is submerged this is a sign that the old life has come to an end. When the candidate is raised from the water we see that a completely new life has begun. The water itself symbolises the washing away of sin. It can also symbolise the pouring out of the Holy Spirit.

Before you come to the group think about the symbolism of bread and wine. What does it mean?

- What does the bread symbolise? In other words what is the meaning of the bread?
- What does the wine symbolise?
- What do we symbolise when we eat and drink the bread and wine?
- What do we symbolise when we do this together? Christians do not remember Jesus in this way on their own.
- Some Christians insist that the bread and the wine must be given to the others by an ordained priest or minister. What is symbolised by this?
- Sometimes you will see a priest formally consecrate the bread and the wine. Why is this?
- Sometimes you will see the priest lift up the consecrated bread and wine before it is distributed to the people. What is the meaning of this action?

You can find the answer to most of these questions on the BBC website (search for 'eucharist').

The New Community

Session 4: Looking back and looking forward

Summary of the session

> When the Christian community meets it is natural to worship God and praise him. Another thing which we often do is to eat bread and drink wine together. We do this to remember Jesus, as he told us to.
>
> By eating bread and drinking wine we look back to the death of Jesus on the cross and allow the cross to speak to us once again. We look forward to the promised return of Jesus and all that this will mean for the future. We renew our commitment to Jesus and to the values of our common life.

Key verse

1 Corinthians 11.26 – 'For as often as you eat this bread and drink the cup, you proclaim the Lord's death until he comes.'

Needed during Session 4

During session four you will be asked to look together at the following passages; each one contains a picture of what will happen when Jesus returns.

> **1 Thessalonians 4.16-17, 1 Corinthians 15.51-53, Mark 8.38 Luke 21.25-27, Matthew 25.31-46**

During the session you will also need the following prayer which the group will pray together after receiving bread and wine:

'Father of all, we give you thanks and praise, that when we were still far off you met us in your Son and brought us home. Dying and living, he declared your love, gave us grace, and opened the gate of glory. May we who share Christ's body live his risen life; we who drink his cup bring life to others; we whom the Spirit lights give light to the world. Keep us firm in the hope you have set before us, so we and all your children shall be free, and the whole earth live to praise your name; through Christ our Lord. **Amen.**'

Exercises following Session 4

Please complete at least one of these four exercises before you come to the next session.

Exercise 1– A communion prayer

Here is a prayer for you to say every day this week.

- Thank you Jesus that you were born as a baby at Bethlehem; God the creator of all things became flesh and blood just as we are flesh and blood. You came to live as we live, and to die as we die. Thank you Jesus that because you were willing to be like us, it is possible for us to become like you, and to have eternal life just as you have. Thank you, Lord Jesus, that by believing in you we have become children of God, just as you are a child of God.

- Thank you Jesus that you submitted yourself to baptism. You were raised from the water of baptism and filled with the Holy Spirit. Throughout your life on earth you looked forward to another baptism when you would die, and then be brought from death to life by the great power of your Father. Thank you that we too have had the privilege of being baptised. Thank you that we too have been filled by the Holy Spirit. Thank you that we too are looking forward to the day of our bodily resurrection.

- Thank you Jesus that you lived by the power of the Holy Spirit, ministering to people on earth. Thank you for all the words that the Spirit gave you to speak. Thank you for all the things you did by the Spirit's power. Thank you that we too have received the Spirit; that we too have been given a number of years in which we can bring the message of the Kingdom to those among whom we live. Thank you that we can speak your words and do the things which you did.

- Thank you Jesus that you chose the cross. Thank you that you suffered on our behalf so that all our sins can be forgiven and forgotten. You have experienced the anger of God in full measure, and because of this we, sinful human beings, are set free. On the cross you defeated sin, defeated Satan, and defeated death, and because of the cross this victory is ours. Thank you that the cross has changed our hearts and become the inspiration for our lives.

- Thank you Jesus that you rose from the grave and were seen alive by many people and on many occasions. Thank you that the power which raised you from the dead is available to us, and that through your resurrection we are able to gain a mastery of ourselves, of all the spiritual forces that come against us, and eventually a mastery of death itself. Thank you that just as you were raised from the dead, we who believe in you will be raised with you.

- Thank you Jesus that you have ascended to the right hand of the Father in heaven. Thank you that all authority in heaven and on earth has been given to you. Thank you Lord that by faith in you we can move mountains. Thank you that we can rely on your protection. Thank you that you are in control of our lives and that nothing can happen to us unless you allow it.

- Thank you Jesus for the promise that you will return to this earth. Thank you that a date for this has been decided and that nothing can stop it. Thank you that the power by which you created the universe will be used again to recreate heaven and earth. Thank you that your return will be followed by judgment and that every wrong will be put right. Thank you that after the judgment there will be an end to sin, to evil, to pain, and to death. Thank you Lord that we have a glorious future, and that we have a reason to live every day.

Exercise 2– Stations of the cross

When we share bread and wine together we are looking back to the death of Jesus on the cross. This exercise encourages us to do that some more.

In some churches you will find, hanging or painted on the walls, fourteen traditional pictures which between them tell the story of the crucifixion. During Lent, Christians look at these pictures in order and meditate on what they see. The pictures are known as the Stations of the Cross. Most are based on things that actually happened, but a few are based on legend. For example, one of the pictures shows a woman called Veronica comforting Jesus as he moved towards his execution – but there is no biblical or historical record of Veronica.

The list of incidents below is a slightly revised version of the Stations of the Cross. In this list there are thirteen stations; all of these incidents actually happened.

1. **Luke 23.13-25** : Jesus is condemned to death
2. **Matthew 27.27-31** : Jesus is abused by the soldiers
3. **Luke 23.26** : Simon is made to carry the cross
4. **Luke 23.27-31** : Jesus speaks to the women of Jerusalem
5. **Luke 23.32-33** : Jesus is nailed to the cross
6. **Luke 23.34** : Jesus prays for forgiveness for his enemies
7. **John 19.23-24** : The soldiers cast lots for his clothes
8. **Luke 23.35-39** : Jesus is mocked
9. **John 19.26-27** : Jesus speaks to his mother
10. **Luke 23.40-43** : The second criminal speaks to Jesus
11. **Matthew 27.46** : Jesus cries out from the cross
12. **John 19.28-30** : Jesus dies
13. **Luke 23.50-55** : Jesus is buried

Jesus is condemned to death and flogged, c 1200 AD, Museu Nacional d'Art de Catalunya.

If you enjoy drawing, find a sketchbook and sketch your impressions of these thirteen stations. Your impressions could be abstract or more literal, as you prefer. It may take you a long time to do them all – but as your drawings are completed bring them to the group and show them what you have done.

If you prefer not to draw, look up the biblical references and imagine the scenes one by one.

Exercise 3 – Looking forward

When we share bread and wine together, we look forward to the return of Jesus. This exercise is a short Bible study on looking forward.

Consider **1 Samuel 17.26**. Notice how the boy David is looking forward to what will be done for him if he takes up the challenge of Goliath. If you had been David would you have been up for the challenge? Would it be worth the risk? Now look at **Luke 6.22-23**. What are the risks that all disciples of Jesus must take? What are the rewards? Is it worth it?

Consider **Acts 7.54-60**. As Stephen is being stoned to death, what is he looking forward to? And where is his confidence? Look back to **Acts 6.8** and read the whole story. How could Stephen have avoided what happened to him? What would you have done?

Consider **2 Timothy 4.6-8**. What will be done for Paul when Jesus appears? How has this conviction affected the way that he has lived his life? Consider also the teaching of Jesus in **Luke 12.41-44**.

Now pray about the way you want to live your life. As you pray think about the Olympic athlete who is looking forward to wearing the crown of victory, and believe that one day Jesus will place the victory crown on your head.

Exercise in preparation for Session 5

Go for a walk by yourself and find somewhere where you can look around you into the distance and into the sky. If necessary, take a short trip by car or bus to such a place. When you get there, find somewhere to sit for a while.

You should have four key verses on the go by now:

1 Corinthians 12.13, Matthew 18.20, 1 Peter 1.14-15, 1 Corinthians 11.26.

Spend a few minutes, half an hour if you have it, meditating on these key verses.

The next two sessions of the course will be about learning to pray. Jesus taught us that when we pray we should begin 'Our Father in heaven.' So as you sit, think about heaven. The one to whom you are praying is not on earth, he is in heaven. Look out into the distance, and then look up into the sky, and take in everything you can see. It was all created by God. But you cannot see heaven; and that is where God is. What does this mean? It means that God is huge, far beyond our imagination. He is far beyond the sun and far beyond the distant horizon.

Now try to take in what Jesus said about God. Jesus said that this God who is the creator of all things is also your Father. You are his son, his daughter. He knows you personally. He loves you very much. He knows, as Jesus said, every hair on your head. He knows the day of your birth and the moment of your death. And, if Jesus is to be believed, he cares about you.

When you have taken in who God is, the God of heaven, the God who is your Father, then start talking to him. Out loud would be good. Every father loves to hear his children talking.

The New Community

Session 5: Learning to pray together

Summary of the session

> Jesus gave his disciples a model for prayer.
>
> He said when you pray, first find a way of giving honour to God, remembering that he is both the great and awesome God of heaven and also the God who has become a Father to you.
>
> Then Jesus said that we should pray for the Kingdom to come. This prayer has many aspects. First we must pray that the Kingdom will come in our own individual lives. This means yielding control of our lives to God, and it means asking to be filled daily by the Holy Spirit.
>
> Jesus demonstrated the Kingdom; wherever he went God reigned and evil, sin, sickness, and death were defeated. Today Jesus is present in the church, including our group, and so we pray for all Christian groups and churches. We pray that they will be filled by righteousness, peace, joy, power and love. These are all signs of the presence of the Kingdom.
>
> Then we pray for those who are involved in spreading the Kingdom throughout the earth. We also pray for our own efforts to reach the people in our own community.
>
> Today there many signs of the Kingdom – places on earth where, for a time at least, God really does rule. But the coming of the Kingdom will not be finally complete until Jesus returns. So when we pray for the Kingdom to come we pray above all that Jesus will come soon.

Key verse for Session 5

Matthew 17.20 – 'Truly I tell you, if you have faith the size of a mustard seed, you will say to this mountain, 'Move from here to there', and it will move; and nothing will be impossible for you.'

Needed during Session 5

During this session you will be asked to pray in pairs, either in your own words or using the prayer below:

'Lord God, our God and King, I pray for my friend Robert. Robert has prayed giving his life to you and welcoming you as his king. I now declare in the name of Jesus that Satan has no place in Robert's life. I command Satan and all his angels to go from Robert's life and to have no authority over him. I place a shield of protection around him in the name of Jesus. I now lay hands on you my brother and pray that once again the Lord will fill you with his Holy Spirit so that you may overflow with power, with joy, with righteousness, and with love.'

During this session you will be asked to look up the following verses, and come up with a list of four words which characterise a Christian community where Jesus is King.

Romans 14.17, 1 Corinthians 4.20, Galatians 5.22-23.

Exercises following Session 5

Exercise 1 – Meditating on John's vision

Repeat the meditation exercise from **Revelation 4** which you did in the session, but this time aim to go right to the end of **Revelation 5**. Devote a few minutes of each day to this exercise, and continue for a week or more.

These chapters are part of a vision that was given to the apostle John by the Holy Spirit, and what you are reading is John's faithful account of what he saw. Sometimes today people still receive visions from God. A vision is a message from God revealed in the form of a vivid picture. If you are praying and you find that you receive a vision or picture, you should look carefully and then report it to others.

This vision that John received has been reported to all Christians in all time through the pages of the Bible. Visions are not easy to interpret, but this vision is important for all of us because it is clearly trying to tell us something about Heaven, the place where God dwells, and something about the future in which we will all one day be caught up. As you read John's vision think about it carefully, and ask the Holy Spirit to speak to you.

On the first day use only the first four verses of chapter four. Imagine the scene bit by bit and take it all in. See the open door to heaven. When you have taken in the open door hear the trumpet sound. Then hear the command to go up through the door. Experience what it is like to be in the Spirit. Then see the throne and contemplate the one who is seated there. See the precious stones and the rainbow. Admire the twenty four elders with their white robes and golden crowns, and think about their role in the government of Heaven. If you take this slowly it will be enough for one day.

The next day go back to the beginning and recover what you experienced yesterday, but this time go a little more quickly so that you have time to press on to the end of verse 6. When you come to verses 5 and 6 focus on the lightning and the thunder, the blazing lamps, and then finally the crystal sea. Then on the next day begin at the beginning again and this time reach to the end of verse 8, or if you prefer go on to the end of chapter four. Each day read a bit further until finally you reach the end of chapter five.

The throne and the elders, by Fra Angelico

Exercise 2 – Praying for the Kingdom to come

Find a quiet place, sit for half an hour, and pray for the Kingdom to come. Perhaps you have never prayed like this before; reflect that this is how Jesus wants you to pray. So ask him to help you to make this prayer well.

First pray for yourself that God's Kingdom may come in your own life. To help you do this, meditate on the following verses.

> Matthew 5.20, Matthew 6.19-21, Matthew 7.21, Mark 9.47
> Mark 10.15, Luke 9.57-62

Next pray for each other that the Kingdom may increase among you. First pray for a greater commitment to righteousness; as you pray for righteousness make your prayer as specific as you can. For example, 'Lord I pray for Vicky as she tries to be a loving wife to a difficult husband.' Then pray for love and peace – 'Lord I pray for John and Mike that they may resolve their differences.' Pray for joy – 'Lord I pray for our meeting that as we sing together you will fill us with joy.' Pray for power – 'Lord I pray that you will heal the pain in Sam's back.'

Then pray for the people God is going to add to your group. Make a list of your neighbours, friends and colleagues. Concentrate your prayer on a few of these names and resolve to continue in prayer until something happens. Begin by praying for an opportunity to come closer to each of them and then pray that each one of them will become curious about your faith.

P U S H – pray until something happens

Now pray for one person who you know has been called to demonstrate the Kingdom. Then pray for another church, perhaps in another city, that it may be filled with signs of the Kingdom. And pray for one person who works as an evangelist in another country. Finally, pray asking that Jesus will return soon. If you have a copy of the CD, sing along to the song 'Maranatha' (track 21).

Exercise 3 – Saints

Since the time of Jesus, many people have given their lives for the sake of the Kingdom. 'Your Kingdom come' has not only been their prayer; it has become their preoccupation, the theme of their whole lives. Mostly these people are not remembered here on earth (though they are remembered in heaven). But in some cases their stories are preserved for us in great detail, and their lives have become an inspiration for many Christians.

Some branches of the Christian church have singled out some of these people and called them saints. The word saint just means 'holy person' – a person whose whole life has been set apart for the Kingdom of God. In the lives of the saints miraculous stories abound. There are many saints in all branches of the Church.

Here is a selection of well known saints about whom we know a great deal. Choose one of them and use the internet or library to find out as much as you can about their lives (try the books listed):

St Francis of Assisi
St Ignatius Loyola
St Patrick of Ireland
St Columba
St Thérèse of Lisieux
John Wesley
Mother Teresa of Calcutta
Brother Yun of China (*The Heavenly Man*)
David Wilkerson (*The Cross and the Switchblade*)
Brother Andrew (*God's Smuggler*)
Gladys Aylward, missionary to China (*The Small Woman* by Alan Burgess)
William Carey
Jim Elliott (*Shadow of the Almighty* by Elizabeth Elliott)
James Hudson Taylor
George Mueller
Mary Slessor

St Francis, a 14th century painting by Andrea Vanni

Exercise in preparation for Session 6

Make a list of all the major items that you possess. What do you think that you are worth in financial terms?

Some people have very few possessions, many are in debt, and some in serious debt. If this applies to you, don't worry about this exercise – but do consider the possibility of getting some help, maybe beginning by sharing your circumstances with the group.

Some people have money and possessions which are surplus to their needs. Some have savings or investments set aside for a rainy day, but which they may never use, and will leave to others in their wills. Some of us have incomes which comfortably exceed necessary expenditure.

If you are one of those with a surplus, offer this surplus to God in prayer and ask him what he wants you to do with it. To help you, consider **Matthew 13.44-45, Matthew 6.19-21,** and **Matthew 19.21.**

The New Community

Session 6: More about prayer

Summary of the session

> The third prayer in the Lord's Prayer asks that God will meet our material needs. Those whose material needs are already well supplied need not pray this prayer; they should thank God for his provision, and then consider their responsibility to give generously from their surplus.
>
> We all have material needs, but we have other needs too. God knows our needs, and whatever they are we should bring them to him in prayer. It is good to be specific in the way in which we ask him to provide for us.
>
> In the Lord's Prayer the fourth request has two parts. First we ask forgiveness for all our sins, and then we ask God to forgive all those who have sinned against us. We should pray this every day, and then the past should be forgotten by us, as it is by God.
>
> Finally we pray about the things in our lives which are putting us under pressure. This is both a prayer of trust in a God who loves us, and it is also a prayer for protection against Satan who seeks to break us.
>
> When we pray we always pray to the Father in the name of Jesus.

Key verse

John 16.24 – 'Until now you have not asked for anything in my name. Ask and you will receive, so that your joy may be complete.'

Needed during Session 6

During session 6 you will need two model prayers. The first is a prayer of forgiveness. The prayer below imagines a person called John who has sinned against you. This is how you should pray for him.

'Father, John has hurt me. I know this is not right and that you are as angry with John as I am. But I ask you, Father, to have mercy on John as you have mercy on me. I ask you to forgive and to help him. Do not hold his sin against him. And help me to see John as you see John – for I know that you love him.'

The second model prayer imagines that you have had a sleepless night and a rough day. This prayer shows how you should pray about this:

'Father I was unable to sleep last night, and today has been a big struggle for me. Father you know that I have much to thank you for, but you and I both know that sometimes things happen where it is hard for me to see your blessing. But despite what has happened I trust you; I trust you that, because you love me, then there must be some good purpose or some way of turning this to good. So Father I praise you for today and for my tiredness and the things I am learning through it. And I praise you for the opportunity to show that I love and trust you. But Lord I also thank you that you will not allow me to be tested beyond my strength. I cannot continue to live with so little sleep, so Lord I pray that you will find a way to enable me to sleep well tonight.'

You will also need this prayer to say together as a group:

'Father you know us. Father you love us. Father you have a plan. Father we will trust you. Father keep us from the evil one today.'

Exercises following Session 6

Exercise 1 – Praying the Lord's Prayer

The Lord's Prayer provides a structure which can be used for daily prayer. Try it out at least once this week. If you follow the instructions it will take you about half an hour.

Father hallowed be thy name

Stand. Close your eyes. Bow your head and ask God to reveal his presence to you. Wait in silence for the Spirit to come to you. Then lift up your hands high in praise to God. Imagine the scene in heaven and join in the prayer and worship. Sing a song of praise with all of your heart. Any song that you know will do. If you have a copy of the course CD use this to help you sing.

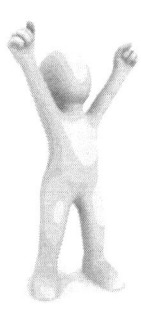

Now kneel in surrender to the King of heaven. Raise your hands out flat in front of you. On your hands place your dreams and place all the people and all the things that you love. Offer them to God.

Then sit and talk to your Father. Tell him about how you are feeling about life. Tell him about your problems. Ask him for his comfort and his counsel.

Your Kingdom come

Choose one aspect of your life, maybe your home, or your place of work, or your church. On a piece of paper write down what this place will look like when the Kingdom comes and Jesus starts to rule. As you write, be prayerful and ask God to give you the precise words. When you have finished writing, ask God to make this happen in every detail. It may seem impossible that your home or your church could ever be as you have described it on the piece of paper but pray that it will be so. God is a god of the impossible.

Give us each day our daily bread

Now write a list of things you plan to do today. Against each item write down one thing that you will need. It might be something like courage, or success, or for hearts to melt. Then pray that your Father will provide for each of these needs.

Forgive us our sins for we ourselves forgive all who have sinned against us

Follow the pattern that you used in the session. Think about yesterday and write down all the things that went wrong. If they were your fault, ask your Father for forgiveness. If others have harmed, upset or wronged you, pray for them, asking your Father to forgive them. If the bad things were just things that happened, then thank God that he has promised that you will never be tested beyond your ability to bear it (**1 Corinthians 10.13**).

Do not bring us to the time of trial

Go back to the list of things that you plan for today. Ask that God's angels will surround you and that you will always have his protection. Turn to **Psalm 91** and, as you read through it, make it your own prayer.

Exercise 2 – Hierarchy of needs

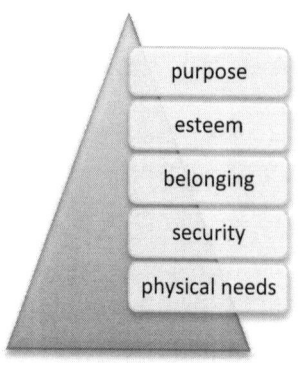

The psychologist Abraham Maslow came up with a pyramid structure for understanding human needs. The most basic of human needs are physical needs, for example air and food. Begin this exercise by asking if all your physical needs are met. If any of them are not, for example if you do not have money to buy food, then pray that God will meet your need.

Maslow's next level of need is the need for security. Ask yourself 'do I feel completely safe or am I in some kind of danger?' If you are in danger, look at **Deuteronomy 33.27**, and ask God to protect you.

The next level of need is belonging. We all have a need to belong somewhere. So are there people who love you and accept you for who you are? Do you have the friends and family that you need? If you have no friends, if you feel like an outsider wherever you go, if you have no one to share your life with, then ask God to provide.

The fourth level is esteem. We all need self-respect, and we all need to be respected by others. We need a role in life in which we feel both fulfilled and valued. Are these needs met for you? If not pray that God will help you.

Finally consider **Proverbs 29.18**. All of us need vision, a sense of what our lives are meant to accomplish, a sense of what is our unique contribution to this world. If your physical needs are all met, if you are in no kind of danger, if you have a loving family and plenty of friends, and if you are well respected and feel good about your abilities, it may still be that in your heart there is a great sense of unease. This will be because, although the first four levels of need are well met, you lack vision or clear purpose. Bring your need to your Father in heaven and keep on praying until God speaks clearly to you about the future.

Exercise 3 – Prayer walking

Go on a prayer walk, either on your own or with a friend. Prayer walks are based on the idea that every aspect of life is in some sense under the influence of Satan, our spiritual enemy (See **1 John 5.19**). The purpose of the prayer walk is to recapture the territory from Satan.

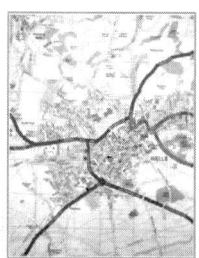

So first decide where to walk. Which piece of territory are you trying to capture for the kingdom? Here are some possibilities:

- Walk around your own home. Go round the boundaries and into each room in turn. Stop and pray in each one. Pray about everything that goes on in that room, and pray for everyone who uses that room. Claim the territory for the Kingdom in the name of Jesus.

- Or walk round and pray for your workplace. In particular, and if appropriate, repent for the sins that are being committed in your workplace and for the ungodly values that prevail there. You are praying on behalf of the people with whom you work, both past and present. Consider **Nehemiah 1.1-11**, where Nehemiah is praying in a similar way on behalf of his nation.

- Walk round your neighbourhood praying for the homes, the schools, the shops, and the churches. As you walk, ask God to lay particular places and people on your heart. And aim to develop a sense of what God plans to do in that area.
- If your church has parish boundaries, walk round those boundaries. Repent of the bad things that are happening within them and praise God for the good things. And pray that God's kingdom will come to that place.
- If you prefer not to walk, use a map as the basis for your prayer. For example you could use a map which shows the cities in England or a map which shows the countries of Africa. Place the map in front of you and pray for each place.

Exercise in preparation for Session 7

Imagine that there is going to be a funeral service. The person who has died is the person who has loved you more than anyone else ever has. Who is this person? In this exercise you will write a speech to be delivered at their funeral service. In  this speech describe the experience of being loved, and include some examples. How did you know that you were loved so much? Was it things that were said? Was it things that were done? Was the love expressed in looks or by touch? What did being loved feel like, and what difference has it made to your life?

Then in a second section to your speech express the love that you feel for this other person. Tell your audience how you feel and what you would have liked to do if more time had been available. If the person you have identified is still alive, consider sending a copy of your speech to them. If they have died, consider sending your speech to those who were close to them and still miss them as much as you do.

The New Community

Session 7: Expressing love for God

Summary of the session

> In earlier sessions we defined worship as bowing down to or honouring God. Now we look at a different dimension to worship. Instead of bowing down to God we approach him with a kiss.
>
> To love God like this we must first experience his love for us. When we experience God's love, fear is driven out of our lives, and we are free to love him.
>
> At times in our lives we all become aware of great needs. God is able to meet our needs; this causes our love for him to increase.
>
> Love for God is often displayed by deeds of commitment and sacrifice on our part. But when we meet as a group we can also express our love for God by singing love songs to him.
>
> Every day we can express our love for God by loving the people around us. By giving ourselves in love to one person after another we are giving ourselves to Jesus.

Key verse

1 John 4.18 – 'There is no fear in love, but perfect love casts out fear; for fear has to do with punishment, and whoever fears has not reached perfection in love.'

Needed during Session 7

Identifying people who love us:

- We love people who give us hugs. Think of someone who gives you lots of hugs. How do you respond to that person?
- We love people who believe in us. Think of someone who believes in you. How do you respond to that person?

- We love people who, although they are important, treat us as if we were just as important as they are. Think of someone who behaves like this.
- We love people who are always there for us. Think of someone who is always there for you, an utterly reliable faithful friend.
- We love people who have made big sacrifices for us. Think of someone who has made sacrifices for you.

When you have shared your answers, go on to these questions:

- Are you used to receiving hugs from God?
- Does God believe in you?
- Does God treat you as important to him?
- Is God there for you? Is he a faithful friend?
- Has God made big sacrifices for you?

Later in the session you will be asked to look at **Luke 7.36-50,** the story of a woman who loved Jesus, and to answer the following questions:

- Why did the woman love Jesus?
- How did she express her love for Jesus?
- If we really loved Jesus, how would we express our love for him?

Exercises following Session 7

Exercise 1– Copying the Good Samaritan

Read the story of the Good Samaritan in **Luke 10.25-37.** In particular notice how in verse 33 the

Samaritan was moved with pity for the unfortunate man. The priest and the Levite in the story represent all those who travel through life without pity, failing to notice the needs of those around them. Your task in this exercise is to journey through the next seven days noticing everyone who crosses your path. Each one of these people matters to God, so let them matter to you. To live with this level of compassion for people will mean living life slowly, much more slowly than usual.

In your home, at your workplace, and as you go on your way, notice people. Make a deliberate choice to look at each one. Some of these people are very important to you, and others much less important. But do not allow yourself to distinguish – to God all these people are important.

Some of them will not notice you or catch your eye. As they pass, pray for them, inviting God's blessing on their lives. Other people will notice you. Smile at them. Say 'hello' or 'good morning'. There may been no reason to stop and talk, but you will be able to communicate warmth, and perhaps receive it too.

If possible stop and talk, if only briefly. Make it your aim to say something encouraging. Send them on their way lifted by their meeting with you. Rely on God to help you know what to say.

Sometimes there will be an opportunity for a longer conversation. In this conversation, make it your aim to listen carefully. Ask yourself what life is like for this person. Stand alongside them. If they are interested, share something of yourself with them. If your faith becomes the subject welcome this and talk about it, but do not try to force it.

With some people it will be possible to offer friendship, to suggest another meeting, to offer hospitality. If you get this opportunity, take it.

Most days you will meet someone who needs your help. Be like the good Samaritan, ready to give the help that is needed.

A prayer by Mother Teresa

To live with this level of compassion for people will mean living life slowly, much more slowly than most people do. This is the way that Mother Teresa lived during her years working in the slums of Calcutta. And this is a prayer which she wrote about her life there. You might like to make this prayer your own.

Oh Jesus,
You who suffer,
Grant that, today and every day,
I may be able to see you in the person of your sick ones,
And that, by offering them my care,
I may serve You.
Grant that, even if you are hidden under the unattractive disguise of
Anger, of crime, or of madness,
I may recognise You and say,
'Jesus, You who suffer, how sweet it is to serve you.'

Give me, Lord, this vision of faith,
And my work will never be monotonous,
I will find joy in harbouring the small whims and desires
Of all the poor who suffer.
Dear sick one, you are still more beloved to me
Because you represent Christ.
What a privilege I am granted in being able to take care of you!

O God, since You are Jesus who suffers,
Deign to be for me also
A Jesus who is patient, indulgent with my faults,
Who looks only at my intentions,
Which are to love you and to serve you
In the person of each of these children of yours who suffer.
Lord, increase my faith.
Bless my efforts and my work, now and forever

Exercise 2 – Becoming like David

Psalm 63 was written by David, the king of Israel. It speaks about the love relationship that existed between David and God. Work your way through the Psalm and try to feel as David felt.

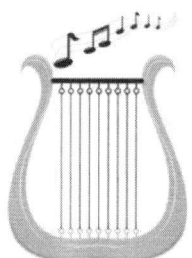

Verse 1 - Sometimes we feel dry, dissatisfied, out of sorts, grumpy, or miles away from God. This is a normal part of the experience of every Christian. But notice that David is not content to remain like that. He wants to feel full of God. He wants to feel close to God. He wants to be surrounded by God's presence. So David expresses his longing for God. Why not do the same? Why not open your mouth and tell God just how much you are missing him? To help you do that have a look at what Jesus promised in **Matthew 11.28-29** and **John 7.37-39**. And if you have a copy of the course CD play track 15 'No one loves me like you love me.'

Verse 2 - David went actively looking for the power and glory of God. Why not do the same? Begin by thinking about the creation and how it displays God's power and glory. Think about the things which you yourself have seen – the sun, the night sky, the oceans, the mountains, thunder and lightning, fire and flood, beautiful rainbows. All these are amazing; but what else have you seen? Then read **John 11.37-44** and imagine the scene. Jesus actually raised Lazarus from the tomb. What power! What glory! What is the most amazing thing which you have seen God do? What is the most amazing thing that you have heard or read about?

Verses 3-4 - David deliberately chooses to praise God and to bless him. You can do the same. Praise God for his attributes; his faithfulness, his holiness, his greatness, his love, his goodness, his power. Bless God for all the blessings that he has poured out into your life. Take a few moments to count your blessings, and as you see how blessed you are, speak out your thanks: 'Bless you God, bless you Lord, bless You Jesus.'

Verses 5-6 - David fed his soul by meditation. He lay on his bed and spent hours thinking about God. You probably don't have hours to lie on your bed; but you do have seven scriptures that you have memorised! Lie down and recall them one by one, pausing to think carefully about each one in turn.

Verses 7-11 - David reflects on his battles and remembers how he always won through, how he was always kept safe, always upheld. You do the same. Reflect on the battles you have had with difficult people, with hard circumstances, with ill health, with temptation. Reflect on how you have trusted God in these things and how he has always been there for you. If a battle is raging for you right now then turn to **Psalm 46.1-3**.

Exercise 3 – Saying 'I love you'

Think of someone to whom you would like to say 'I love you'. This should be someone you really do love, but who might not fully realise that you do. First think about how this person usually expresses love. When they want to communicate love, how do they do it? What language do they use? Do they show affection? Give gifts? Find ways to take pressure off others? Speak out their love in words?

Once you have understood your loved one's language of love, do something extravagant to express your love for them, making sure you use their language. If your loved one likes to give gifts, choose a gift for them, but choose very carefully and spend enough to get your message across. If they like to use affirming words , then use affirming words to them. If they like to show loyalty, show loyalty to them.

Now do something extravagant for Jesus. Here are some suggestions:

- Give a lot of money to the poor, perhaps to an individual or perhaps to a charity. Don't tell anyone you are doing this. But tell Jesus that this gift is for him.

- Think of a person who is lonely, and plan to spend some of your time on this person. Take them on a trip. Invite them to your house. Pay them a visit and take a gift. Jesus said 'whatever you do for the least of my brothers, you do for me.'

- Plan to take a week of your annual holiday and look for a way to spend this week serving Jesus.

- Go to see your church leader and offer your time to serve the mission of the church in any way that is needed.
- Spend a whole evening (or even a whole night) in prayer and praise to God

Don't do any of these things as a duty or a penance; do them because you love Jesus and because you want to.

Exercise in preparation for Session 8

The extraordinary thing is that the great and almighty God, the creator of the universe, sometimes chooses to speak person to person with human beings like you. Here are four short exercises to help you listen to him. They can be done one after another or on four different days.

Before you begin each exercise ask God to speak to you, and before you end make a note of anything that you hear God say.

For the first exercise read the first nine verses of **1 Peter 1**. Then reread them slowly and carefully. If you find that God is speaking to you, then slow right down. Concentrate on the verse you are looking at and listen carefully. Ask, 'what are you saying to me Lord – please make it plain?'

Next take yourself to a church service. Sing the songs, pray the prayers, listen to the sermon, but all the time listen for God's voice. If God speaks, stop, cut yourself off from what is happening, and be still.

On the way home from church stop somewhere and look around you. Examine the sky, the birds, the animals, the plants, the flowers, the trees. Ask God to speak to you through what you see. Finally, when you get home, find a quiet place and listen to God in the silence. Don't say anything. Just ask him to speak to you. Do this for at least ten minutes; do not give up after a few seconds!

The New Community

Session 8: The power of words

Summary of the session

> God is a God of words. When God speaks something always happens. For example, when God spoke the world was created.
>
> One way we know Jesus is God is that when Jesus spoke things also happened. He said 'Be still', and the wind went away. He said 'Come out,' and the dead man appeared.
>
> Sometimes God speaks directly to the human heart, and when he does the nature of that heart is revealed. Some recognise God's word and it does a great work in their lives. Others are apparently deaf. God speaks to the human heart in many different ways; through creation, people, prophecy, the Bible, and above all through Jesus.
>
> God speaks particularly clearly through the Bible. The Bible is the word of God in two senses: first in the sense that God originally spoke it into being, and second in that he speaks to us as we read it today.
>
> The Bible also has human authorship. Some parts of the Bible were originally written as history but other parts are story, poetry, law, prophecy. The human authors were inspired, but because they were human they are not infallible; God used them in spite of their humanness.
>
> We are to hear God's word, receive it, and be changed by it. But we are also meant to become channels of God's word to others. We do this by the power of our lives, by exposing people to our life together, by sharing the message of the Gospel, and by the power of our prayers.

Key verse

Hebrews 4.12 – The word of God is living and active, sharper than any two-edged sword, piercing until it divides soul from

spirit, joints from marrow; it is able to judge the thoughts and intentions of the heart.

Needed during Session 8

1. Look at **John 1.1-5,** and answer the following questions:

- In this passage who or what is the word of God?
- To whom was this word spoken?
- How was this word spoken?
- What happened as a result?

2. Look up these verses, and try to see what Jesus believed about the Old Testament:

- **Matthew 5.17**
- **Mark 12.10**
- **Matthew 19.4-6**
- **Matthew 22.29**

In the last three of these we see Jesus in the midst of controversy. He uses the Old Testament scriptures to add authority to what he is saying and to prove his opponents wrong.

Now look at **Matthew 4.1-11**, where we see Jesus experiencing temptation. Notice that each time he is tempted Jesus replies with a direct quote from the Book of Deuteronomy.

Exercises following Session 8

Exercise 1– The value of scripture

In **2 Timothy 3.16** Paul writes to his colleague Timothy that everything we read in the Bible is the word of God. This is true in three senses:

1. It is true that God originally inspired the writing of the whole Bible.

2. The Bible is a reliable guide to what is true and what is false – in particular it teaches us the truth about Jesus.

3. God uses the Bible to teach us how to live; indeed the Bible often speaks change into our lives as we are convicted by something we read and take up the challenge to redirect our lives along a path that pleases God.

Meditate again on the eight key verses you have learned so far on this course. Find a pen and paper, and for each verse make a note of all the truths it contains – truth about God, about yourself, about people in general, about the world, about the future. Highlight any truths that have been impressed on your mind as you have been meditating on these verses in recent weeks. How have the verses changed the way you think? What do you believe now that you did not believe when the course began?

Secondly, make a note of how each of the key verses might be used by God to change the way in which someone is living. Highlight examples of scriptures which have influenced the way you have been living in recent weeks.

Exercise 2 – The tools of your trade

In **2 Timothy 3.17** Paul is telling Timothy that the scriptures are to become tools of his trade. Someone who wants to be a man or woman of God and become active in ministry, needs to be equipped with the scriptures.

Choose one person, a Christian whom you know trusts and loves you. Your task is to share one of the scriptures you have learned with this person. You must decide which scripture. Arrange to see your friend and ask if they'd be happy for you to share one of the scriptures which you have been learning. Then share what the scripture is, what it has meant to you, what you have learned from it, and how your life has changed. Then ask if that makes sense to your friend and if there is any way in which this scripture speaks to them or ever has spoken to them. This will probably lead you into a deep conversation and an opportunity to pray for one another.

Now that you have done this once, be on the lookout for more opportunities to share your scriptures. As you go about your life, and meet and talk with people, it will sometimes occur to you that this person needs one or other of the truths contained in the verses you have learned. Whenever this happens, ask for permission to share something from the Bible. If the person is agreeable:

- Open the Bible and find the verse
- Ask your friend to read the verse aloud
- Ask them what they think the verse is saying
- Share how you personally have found it to be helpful
- Ask if the verse speaks to the need that your friend has
- Pray together

Exercise 3 – Becoming the word of God to others

In the session you learned that you can be the word of God to other people. This can happen in any of four ways.

- **Matthew 5.16**: The way that we live speaks, and this will lead to change in the way that others see God. If we are living close to God, we can be completely confident that our lives are going to have a powerful impact.

- **John 13.34-35**: The way that Christians love each other speaks. God speaks as we allow people to see the life that we are enjoying together in our church or our group. We can be confident that when non-Christians see us together and see our love, power, joy and righteousness, many of them will be drawn to look for the source of our life.

- **Romans 1.16**: We speak to people by sharing a message – the message about Jesus. We can be confident that this message of the gospel has great power to change lives.

- **Acts 3.6**: We speak directly to the disorders in people's lives in the name of Jesus. For example, if someone is sick, we offer to pray. When people see the power of our prayers, they will be drawn towards faith in Jesus, the source of that power.

Make a list of four non-Christians whom you know and love. Pray for each one, asking God to direct you to one of these four actions:

- Say nothing, but continue to witness to Jesus by the way that you live day by day. But also pray that the time will come when your friend will begin to ask questions about the reason why you live in the way that you do.

- Invite your friend to spend an evening with the group. This could be a social evening or a normal group meeting. Explain to your friend that you belong to the group, explain what it does when it meets, and ask if he or she would like to come to one of the meetings.

- Invite your friend to a meeting where you know that the gospel will be explained. Or explain the gospel to them yourself! Begin by asking if they understand what the Christian message is, and if they would like you to explain it to them.

- Perhaps your friend has a problem, for example an illness, which they cannot solve by themselves. You know that when you have problems like this you always bring them to God. Tell your friend that, and ask if he or she would like you to pray. Say it does not matter if they are a believer – what matters is that you are, and that your experience since you became a Christian is that you have been given authority from God to deal with such matters.

Exercise in preparation for Session 9

This exercise is about vision. You have vision when you can describe the future as you hope it will be.

Lots of people have vision; parents have vision for what they hope their children will be, architects draw pictures of buildings they hope to see go up, businessmen have vision for companies they hope to develop. Vision is usually a good thing to have because it determines the direction in which you must travel.

Some vision is just wishful thinking, but the best kind of vision is that which has been given to us by God. If God ever says to us 'this is what is going to happen,' then we can press ahead confident that what God has promised he will fulfil.

A good question to ask someone is, 'What would you like to be doing in ten years' time?' When we ask this question the answer is often very revealing, telling us a lot about how the other person sees their life. It also tells you whether or not they have any vision.

So ask yourself the same question 'What would I like to be doing in ten years' time?' If you know the answer, and you know that God is behind that answer, you are in a good place.

Even so this question is not the most important question. This is because as Christians we have to learn to think of ourselves not just as individuals but as part of a group. So ask yourself the question 'Where would I like our group to be in ten years' time? Where would I like the group to be in one year's time?' When you know the answer, share it with the others by email, text or on Facebook. Once the whole group gains a sense of where you are all going together, you will find that you have a sense of unity and a heart of strength. The group will have vision.

Don't neglect to do this. If the whole group, or most of you, go for this exercise you will find that it will take you to a new place.

The New Community

Session 9: A community of love

Summary of the session

> Before the creation of the world, love existed – a love between the Father, the Son, and the Spirit. Christian fellowship is about being caught up into this pre-existing love.
>
> Whenever a Christian community is formed, then Father, Son and Spirit are present in that community. This is revealed in many ways, but primarily in the love that the members of the community have for one other.
>
> One aspect of Christian love is compassion. Your sorrow is my sorrow, your joys are my joys. I feel with you. Listening is part of compassion. As we listen, the Spirit enables us to identify with the person speaking.
>
> As we listen to each other we should also listen to the Holy Spirit. The Spirit shows us how to bring comfort, guidance, healing, change, or whatever is needed.
>
> As we listen to the Spirit together, the Spirit gives wisdom, knowledge, faith, discernment, prophecy, healings, miracles, or tongues as they are needed. No one person has all these gifts – it is a team effort.

Key verse

1 John 4.11 – 'Beloved, since God loved us so much, we also ought to love one another.'

Needed during Session 9

Look at the following verses, and see just how deep Christian fellowship is meant to be: **Acts 2.44-46, 1 John 3.16-18, Galatians 5.13-15**

Exercises following Session 9

Exercise 1– Praying in the Spirit

In an earlier exercise it was suggested that you compile a collection of photographs of the group members. This exercise is about having compassion for each of the group members, and you will find that it is easier to do that if you are able to look at their faces.

As you look at the faces ask the Holy Spirit to give you a great love for each person, and wait until your heart becomes engaged. It should amaze you to think that God loves this person so much that he gave his own Son to die for them. Ask the Holy Spirit to make you willing to die too, or to do anything for him or her that may be needed.

Now ask to be given insight into how this person is feeling right now. Are they happy or sad? Are they angry or peaceful? Do they feel secure or are they afraid? Is anything worrying them? As you begin to get a sense of how the person is feeling ask for the gift of compassion that you may be able to feel as they feel.

Now listen to the Holy Spirit for each person in turn, and remember what you learned in the session about spiritual gifts.

- Do you have wisdom or insight that could be helpful? If so, ask the Lord if you should share it. Anything you do decide to communicate should be in person, not by text or email.

- Did any information or knowledge come to you as you prayed? If so, share it with the person concerned. Just say 'I was praying for you the other day and a picture formed in my mind, or a verse of scripture came to me, or I saw you surrounded by children,' or whatever. Then ask if this makes sense.

- Do you have faith to pray with confidence for something to happen in this person's life? Don't necessarily share it – just keep on praying.

- Is this person sick? If you are confident that God wants to heal, then offer to pray for him or her.

- Is a miracle needed? Plan to get together with others and pray for one.

- Is the Spirit giving you a word from God which you must share with this person? Remember that such words are never negative. Their purpose is to encourage, to build up, or to stir up.

- Do you think after praying that there is a deeper, perhaps spiritual reason, behind the problems that this person has? You should be cautious about sharing this – better to bide your time and wait to see if anything confirms what you are thinking.

- If you have the gift of tongues, use it as you pray. If you do not have the gift, then ask God for it. This gift is usually given quite unexpectedly. Other than asking for it, there is nothing you can do to make it happen.

When you have finished praying for a person, send them a message which says 'I have been praying for you today and thanking God for you because...... and I wanted to let you know that I love you.'

Exercise 2 – Evangelism through love

Begin by reading **John 13.34-35**. In verse 34 Jesus is teaching his disciples that they should love each other. All effective Christians belong to Christian communities, in which they undertake to love the other members as they love their own brothers and sisters.

In verse 35 Jesus explains that the love we have for each other will have a spin-off. If we love each other, people will notice. God's plan is for Christians to form communities which are so full of love that anyone looking in from the outside will be attracted to join without a word being spoken.

So think of a way of mixing up your Christian friends and your non-Christians friends and see what happens. First make a list of your non-Christian friends; limit this list to people you see regularly. Pray over the list and try to identify one person whom you long to see become a Christian. Suppose this person's name is Ruth. Now make a list of your Christian friends and pray over this list. From this list identify someone you know really loves you. Suppose this person's name is Katy.

Now all you have to do is to work out a way of bringing yourself, Ruth and Katy together – not to talk about God, but just to have some fun together. Maybe you will want to make a bigger party than just the three of you, but make sure that Katy and Ruth are both included. It may be that Katy will end up talking to Ruth about her faith, and it may be that this won't happen. The important thing is to include Ruth in the love that you and Katy share.

Exercise 3 – Spirit-led conversations

Turn to **John 4.4-26** and read the story. Jesus was passing through Samaria, and he was resting after a hard day of walking. A woman appeared. She was a Samaritan, and Jews never spoke to Samaritans. She was a woman, and men never spoke in public to women. So the natural thing for Jesus to do would be to ignore her.

But Jesus did not ignore her. He had compassion for her – he felt for her; he was concerned for her.
He spoke to her, asking her for some water. This week copy Jesus. Wherever you go, speak to people you don't have to speak to. As Jesus did, open up the conversation in a matter of fact way.

Now read the story again from verse 9, and you will see how the conversation developed. The woman speaks six times, and Jesus responds six times. Look at the six things that the woman said and the six things that Jesus said.

You will have noticed that the things Jesus said got to the heart of the matter with remarkable speed. You may have wondered how Jesus did it. The answer is that at the same time as he was listening to the woman, Jesus was also listening to the Holy Spirit. This is obvious in verse 18 where the Holy Spirit gives Jesus the knowledge that the woman had had five husbands and five divorces.

So as you speak to people this week listen to what they say very carefully, but also try to listen to the Holy Spirit at the same time, and ask him what to say next. You too may find that you get to the heart of the matter much more quickly than you would have done without the Spirit's help.

Exercise in preparation for Session 10

Read **Ephesians 3.14-21**, which is a prayer by St Paul for a group of Christians in Ephesus – a group which would have had many similarities to your own group. Notice, from **verses 14-15**, the earnestness with which Paul prays and, from **verses 20-21**, the confidence he has that his prayer will be answered.

...the breadth and length and height and depth of the love of Christ...

Now look at **verses 16-19**, which give the content of Paul's prayer. Write a similar prayer about your own group, but in your own words. When you are happy with the prayer you have written, get down on your knees as Paul did, and pray your prayer out loud. Then, if you use email, send a copy of your prayer to the other members of the group.

Now look at the first three verses of **chapter 4**. Despite the earnestness of his prayer, and despite his confidence in God, Paul knows that his great prayer will only become a reality in Ephesus if the Ephesian Christians co-operate with the Holy Spirit. This co-operation involves five things:

- Humility
- Gentleness
- Patience
- Willingness to bear with one another
- Eagerness for unity

It will be the same for your group; if the people in your group demonstrate these five qualities, then the things that Paul prayed for, and you have just prayed for, are going to happen in your group just as they did long ago in Ephesus.

So think for a while what might be required of you. To help you do this, ask yourself the following questions.

- Who in my group is competitive or full of themselves?
- Who in the group needs gentle handling?
- Who in the group is slow to understand and to change?
- Who in the group is annoying?
- Who in the group is it hard to see eye to eye with?

Maybe the answer to all five of these questions is no one. But more likely there will be someone, or perhaps several people. If so, ask the Holy Spirit to give you the grace to demonstrate humility, gentleness, patience, forbearance, and eagerness for unity.

The New Community

Session 10: More about loving each other

Summary of the session

> One aspect of love between Christians is kindness. To be kind to someone means to treat them as a brother or a sister, a member of your own family.
>
> Another aspect of Christian love is humility. In the world people compete with each other. In the church we promote each other. In the church we try to ensure that each person has a role which is appropriate for them and fulfils them. Some possible roles are prophet, servant, teacher, exhorter, giver, leader, bringer of compassion.
>
> Meekness is another aspect of love. I am meek towards God if I listen to his every word, and obey without question. I am meek towards you if I gladly accept your ministry in my life.
>
> Within the church, or the group, we have to learn to be patient with those among us who are slow to learn or change, to accept those who we find difficult, and to forgive those who treat us badly.
>
> If wrong things happen in the fellowship they should not be covered up but talked through. We are to value both righteousness and peace.

Key verse

Luke 17.3-4 – 'Be on your guard! If another disciple sins, you must rebuke the offender, and if there is repentance, you must forgive. And if the same person sins against you seven times a day, and turns back to you seven times and says, 'I repent', you must forgive.'

Exercises following Session 10

Exercise 1 – Your nearest and dearest

Make a list which consists first of all the members of your immediate family: parents, children, brothers and sisters; and grandparents, aunts, uncles too if you see them often. Add to this list all the members of your group, who are your spiritual brothers  and sisters. This is a list of your nearest and dearest. You will see these people in a different way to all other people. Your happiness will depend on the success of your relationships with them.

Think your way through this list. Are there some people on the list who are absolutely wonderful – when you think of them your heart fills with joy, for they bring to your life endless good things? Pray for these people with a heart filled with gratitude.

Most of us do have some people on our 'absolutely wonderful' list, but sadly, experience shows that many of our nearest and dearest are not really like that. The success of family life depends on how we handle not the wonderful people, but the others. The same applies in church life.

So concentrate next on those among your nearest and dearest who are the most difficult. **First**, is there anyone on your list who treats you badly? Consider **Matthew 18.21-22**. You have to forgive them, probably on a daily basis. So get down on your knees and ask the Father to forgive and bless them.

Once you have forgiven them, you must decide if anything else needs to be done:

- If the matter is trivial, forgive and forget it.

- If the matter is really serious – one of your nearest and dearest has done something really bad – then confront them; being passive will only make things worse. Follow the procedure outlined by Jesus in **Matthew 18.15-17**. Notice that the worst outcome envisaged by Jesus is that we end up by having to mentally cross that person off our nearest and dearest list. We are not supposed to spend the rest of our lives trying to resolve this issue.

- Some matters are trivial and best forgotten, others serious and best confronted. But there are also some things which are harder to categorise. Don't be one of those people who always confronts or who always lets things go. Instead ask God for wisdom. Look at **Proverbs 9.8**. The rule of thumb is: 'if the person is a fool then let it go; if the person is wise then confront.' This last case is covered by Jesus in **Luke 17.3 & 4**.

Next ask yourself 'Is there anyone among my nearest and dearest who is off the rails?' Sometimes people have 'blind spots' – they are doing something wrong or stupid, and if they do not stop they will suffer for it. If you have anyone like this in your family or your church, look at **Galatians 6.9-10**. Take your concerns to a senior and wise member of the family, or church, and see if they agree. If they do, go together to the person who is struggling and see what can be done to help them.

Finally is there anyone on your list who just annoys you? It is not that they are doing anything wrong, but perhaps there is a personality clash or some trying habits. At any rate you find it difficult to get on with this person. You saw in the session that here you need a combination of patience and forbearance. So pray for these people, and earnestly desire God's grace for yourself so that you may be able to live with them. Remember that, as you find them difficult, they probably also find you difficult; pray that God will one day give a breakthrough so that the relationship becomes a rewarding one for both of you.

Exercise 2 – Loving unlovely people

You have learned in the last two sessions that the ideal for any group of Christians is that they should excel at loving one another. You belong to a group of Christians; your responsibility is to be committed to them, to sacrifice for them, to encourage them, to be compassionate, kind, humble, meek, patient and forgiving. If you and the others behave like this you will have an amazing group.

This ideal of a community full of love is not just a dream; it can and often does become a reality. This is because the Holy Spirit is involved in the group. The Holy Spirit is not just telling you but also helping you to love the others, even the most difficult ones. And the Holy Spirit is also telling each one of them to love you. There are many examples of Christian groups and churches where you can see this mutual love at work.

The problem is that when we move away from our Christian group, life is likely to be much less easy. In your work place, or your leisure club, or wherever you spend time, the chances are that you are not experiencing a community filled by love – sometimes exactly the opposite. The Holy Spirit may be at work in you, but the problem is that the Holy Spirit is not yet inside those other people. So it happens that many Christians experience harmony at church, but disharmony at work, or at home, or in other places.

What are we supposed to do about this? Some Christians handle this by looking for a way to live their entire lives in the church, perhaps by giving up secular work to find employment in a Christian organisation. Sometimes this is the right thing to do; if God calls you this way go ahead. But be very careful lest you be guilty of escapism. Have a look at **Luke 5.29-32**, and you will see Jesus enjoying the company of sinners. It seems that the normal Christian calling is to live with one foot firmly placed in the world even as we are learning to plant the other foot in the church.

So the purpose of this exercise is for you to go out into the world (particularly into your home and workplace) and try to love people there in exactly the same way that we love the people in our churches. This is of course going to be much more difficult; it is hard to love people who don't love you. But see what Jesus said about this in **Matthew 5.43-48**.

So think about your world outside the church and about the people you meet there.

- Is there someone who needs your compassion but never returns it? Resolve to go on listening and caring, and pray for a breakthrough.
- Is there someone who needs you to be kind, but is not kind to you? Try redoubling your efforts to give kindness. Buy them a drink. Buy them a birthday present. Invite them to a party.
- Is there someone who sees you as a rival? Can you humble yourself and bring yourself to build up this person in the eyes of others?
- Is there a difficult boss in your workplace? This is your opportunity to demonstrate meekness.
- Is there a slow person with whom it is hard to be patient?
- Is there an annoying person you can learn to accept?
- Is there a person who has treated you badly, and who you must forgive?

Once you have identified these people pray for them, and for the grace to love them as Jesus loved sinners.

Exercise 3 – Scripture memory

Book 2 of *The God Who is There* is now at an end, and this would be a good time to consolidate your attempts to memorise scripture.

You have learned, or should have learned, ten scriptures from this book:

1 Corinthians 12.13
For in the one Spirit we were all baptised into one body – Jews or Greeks, slaves or free – and we were all made to drink of one Spirit.

Matthew 18.20
For where two or three are gathered in my name, I am there among them.

1 Peter 1.14–15
Like obedient children, do not be conformed to the desires that you formerly had in ignorance. Instead, as he who called you is holy, be holy yourselves in all your conduct.

1 Corinthians 11.26
For as often as you eat this bread and drink the cup, you proclaim the Lord's death until he comes.

Matthew 17.20
He said to them, 'Because of your little faith. For truly I tell you, if you have faith the size of a mustard seed, you will say to this mountain, "Move from here to there", and it will move; and nothing will be impossible for you.'

John 16.24
Until now you have not asked for anything in my name. Ask and you will receive, so that your joy may be complete.

1 John 4.18
There is no fear in love, but perfect love casts out fear; for fear has to do with punishment, and whoever fears has not reached perfection in love.

Hebrews 4.12
The word of God is living and active, sharper than any two-edged sword, piercing until it divides soul from spirit, joints from marrow; it is able to judge the thoughts and intentions of the heart.

1 John 4.11
Beloved, since God loved us so much, we also ought to love one another.

Luke 17.3-4
Be on your guard! If another disciple sins, you must rebuke the offender, and if there is repentance, you must forgive. And if the same person sins against you seven times a day, and turns back to you seven times and says, "I repent", you must forgive.

Have you developed a good system of memorising these verses? If not, go back to session 1, exercise 1 and repeat the exercise.

Exercise in preparation for Book 3

Book 2 of this course has been mainly about life in the church or in the group. Book 3 is mainly about life in the world.

The first session of Book 3 tackles the subject of work. Work is defined everything that keeps life going, so it includes digging the garden and preparing meals as well as the paid work you do.

To prepare for the first session of Book 3 do a piece of work. Choose something that you have to do quite often. Make sure that you do this piece of work quite badly. Do it when you are tired. Don't allow enough time. Cut corners and don't check anything. Play loud music at the same time. Take the approach that any old thing will do.

Now, on another day, do the same piece of work again, but this time do it to the best of your ability. Allow enough time. Check everything. Have high standards. When you have finished ask yourself if this feels better or worse than the first time.

Finally, on yet another day, do the same piece of work again. But this time deliberately turn your work into a prayer. Pray before you start. Talk to God about it as you go along. Ask for his advice, ask for his help, and when the job is complete present it to him for his approval. Did working this way make any difference?

Song Words

and copyright permissions

1. He who appoints
2. I stand in awe
3. You are a holy God
4. How great thou art
5. He is Lord
6. Surrender
7. Blessed be your name
8. Jesus we enthrone you
9. Holy and anointed one
10. Purify my heart
11. Grateful
12. Be still
13. This is the air I breathe
14. Lord have mercy
15. No one loves me like you love me
16. You chose the cross
17. When I survey
18. Jesus all for Jesus
19. Timeless words
20. God in my living
21. Maranatha

1. He who appoints

the sun to shine by day
He who decrees the moon to shine by night
He who has stirred the sea
and calms the storm
He who is called 'I AM' knows me by name

He is Lord, He is Lord
He is Lord, He is Lord of all

He who assigns the autumn leaves to fall
He who commands the snow
to brighten the dawn
He who has called a barren land to birth
He who is called 'I AM' redeems the world

We give
Glory, glory to the Lord God Almighty
Glory to the great I AM

Rich White, Ben Judson, Lauren Keenan
©2010

3. You are a holy God

An all consuming fire
You're robed in majesty
Bright shining as the sun

Your ways are not my ways
Your thoughts are high above
You are the fountain, Lord
Of mercy, truth and love

(and we cry)
Holy, holy is the Lord God most high
(and we cry)
Holy, holy is the Lord God most high

Brian Duane & Kathryn Scott ©1999
Vineyard Songs (UK/Eire) Copycare

2. Who can know

The mind of our Creator?
Who can speak
Of wonders yet unseen?
Who can reach
The height of understanding
To play the notes
Of wisdom's melody?

Who has weighed
The dust of every mountain?
Who has walked
The mysteries of the deep?
Who has laid the earth
On its foundation
And who conducts
The waves upon the sea?

I stand in awe of You
I stand in awe of You
So glorious and true
I stand in awe
I stand in awe

You have seen
The end from the beginning
You have been
Before the world began
You have reached
To me within my darkness
And in the light of mercy
Now I see

Martyn Layzell ©2005 Thankyou Music

4. O Lord my God

When I in awesome wonder
Consider all the works
Thy hand hath made
I see the stars,
I hear the mighty thunder
Thy power throughout
The universe displayed

Then sings my soul,
My Saviour God to Thee
How great Thou art!
How great Thou art!
Then sings my soul,
My Saviour God to Thee
How great Thou art!
How great Thou art!

When through the woods
And forest glades I wander
And hear the birds
Sing sweetly in the trees
When I look down
From lofty mountain grandeur
And hear the brook,
And feel the gentle breeze

And when I think
That God His Son not sparing
Sent Him to die –
I scarce can take it in
That on the cross
My burden gladly bearing
He bled and died
To take away my sin

When Christ shall come
With shout of acclamation
And take me home
What joy shall fill my heart!
Then shall I bow
In humble adoration
And there proclaim,
My God, how great Thou art!

Stuart K Hine ©1953 Thankyou Music

5. He is Lord, He is Lord

He is risen from the dead
And He is Lord
Every knee shall bow
Every tongue confess
That Jesus Christ is Lord

You are Lord, You are Lord
You are risen from the dead
And You are Lord
Every knee shall bow
Every tongue confess
That Jesus Christ is Lord

You're my Lord, You're my Lord
You are risen from the dead
And You're my Lord
And my knee shall bow
And my tongue confess
That Jesus, You're my Lord

Anon

6. I'm giving You my heart

And all that is within
I lay it all down
For the sake of You, my King
I'm giving You my dreams
I'm laying down my rights
I'm giving up my pride
For the promise of new life

And I surrender all to You, all to You
And I surrender all to You, all to You

I'm singing You this song
I'm waiting at the cross
And all the world holds dear
I count it all as loss
For the sake of knowing You
The glory of Your name
To know the lasting joy
Even sharing in Your pain

Marc James ©2000 Vineyard Songs
(UK/Eire) Copycare

7. Blessed be Your name

In the land that is plentiful
Where Your streams
Of abundance flow
Blessed be Your name
Blessed be Your name
When I'm found in the desert place
Though I walk
Through the wilderness
Blessed be Your name

Every blessing You pour out
I'll turn back to praise
When the darkness closes in, Lord
Still I will say

Blessed be the name of the Lord
Blessed be Your name
Blessed be the name of the Lord
Blessed be Your glorious name

Blessed be Your name
When the sun's shining down on me
When the world's
All as it should be
Blessed be Your name
Blessed be Your name
On the road marked with suffering
Though there's pain in the offering
Blessed be Your name

Every blessing You pour out
I'll turn back to praise
When the darkness closes in
Still I will say

You give and take away
You give and take away
My heart will choose to say
Lord blessed be Your name

Matt Redman ©2002 Thankyou music

8. Jesus, we enthrone You

We proclaim You our King
Standing here in the midst of us
We raise You up with our praise

And as we worship, build a throne
And as we worship, build a throne
And as we worship, build a throne
Come, Lord Jesus, and take Your place

Paul Kyle ©1980 Thankyou Music

9. Jesus, Jesus

Holy and anointed One, Jesus
Jesus, Jesus
Risen and exalted One, Jesus

Your name is like honey on my lips
Your Spirit like water to my soul
Your word is a lamp unto my feet
Jesus, I love You, I love You

John Barnett ©1988 Mercy
Publishing/Thankyou Music

10. Purify my heart

Let me be as gold and precious silver
Purify my heart
Let me be as gold, pure gold

Refiner's fire, my heart's one desire
Is to be holy, set apart for You, Lord
I choose to be holy
Set apart for You, my Master
Ready to do Your will

Purify my heart
Cleanse me from within
And make me holy
Purify my heart
Cleanse me from my sin, deep within

Brian Doerksen ©1990 Mercy Publishing/Thankyou Music

11. Grateful for Your death

Upon the tree
Grateful for the life it's given me
Grateful I wasn't turned away
Grateful You invited me to stay

Right here close to You, by Your side
Face to face, eye to eye
Sharing in Your purposes
Seeking out Your will
Learning how to know Your voice
Learning how to follow You

Grateful You lift me when I fall
Grateful You don't condemn at all
Grateful for love so freely shared
Grateful my heart
Has been prepared

To be close to You, by Your side
Face to face, eye to eye
Sharing in Your suffering
Sharing in Your joy
Walking step by step in time
Learning how to follow You.

Phil Lawson Johnston ©2001 IQ Music/Cloud Music

12. Be still for the presence of the Lord

The Holy One is here.
Come, bow before Him now,
With reverence and fear.
In Him no sin is found,
We stand on holy ground.
Be still, for the presence of the Lord,
The Holy One is here.

Be still, for the glory of the Lord,
Is shining all around;
He burns with holy fire,
With splendour He is crowned.
How awesome is the sight,
Our radiant King of light!
Be still, for the glory of the Lord,
Is shining all around.

Be still, for the power of the Lord,
Is moving in this place,
He comes to cleanse and heal,
To minister His grace.
No work too hard for Him,
In faith receive from Him;
Be still, for the power of the Lord,
Is moving in this place.

David Evans© Thankyou Music, 1986

13. This is the air I breathe
This the air I breathe
Your holy presence living in me
This is my daily bread
This is my daily bread
Your very word spoken to me

And I, I'm desperate for You
And I, I'm lost without You

Marie Barnett ©1995 Mercy/Vineyard Publishing

14. Jesus, I've forgotten
The words that You have spoken
Promises that burned within
My heart have now grown dim
With a doubting heart I follow
The paths of earthly wisdom
Forgive me for my unbelief
Renew the fire again

*Lord have mercy
Christ have mercy
Lord have mercy on me*

I have built an altar
Where I worship things of man
I have taken journeys
That have drawn me far from You
Now I am returning
To Your mercies ever flowing
Pardon my transgressions
Help me love You again

I have longed to know You
And Your tender mercies
Like a river of forgiveness
Ever flowing without end
I bow my heart before You
In the goodness of Your presence
Your grace forever shining
Like a beacon in the night.

Steve Merkel ©2000 Integrity's Hosanna! Music

15. No one loves me like You love me
No one knows me like You know me
No one sees me as You see me
Jesus, I am Yours

You have searched me and You know me
You know the places that I go
You know my words before I speak them
O, this is all too wonderful

Where can I go from Your Spirit?
There's no place too far away
Even the darkness cannot hide me
For to You the night is bright as day

It was You who formed and made me
You knew me in the secret place
Your eyes beheld my unformed being
You have written all my days

O how great are all You thoughts, Lord
Beyond the reason of my mind
How vast the sum, I try to count them
But they are more than all the sand.

Ruth Fazal ©Tributary Music 2001

16. You chose the cross
With every breath
The perfect life, the perfect death
You chose the cross
A crown of thorns You wore for us
And crowned us with eternal life
You chose the cross

And though Your soul
Was overwhelmed with pain
Obedient to death, You overcame

I'm lost in wonder, I'm lost in love
I'm lost in praise for evermore
Because of Jesus' unfailing love
I am forgiven, I am restored

You loosed the cords of sinfulness
And broke the chains of my disgrace
You chose the cross
Up from the grave victorious
You rose again so glorious
You chose the cross

The sorrow that surrounded You

Was mine
"Yet not my will
But Yours be done" You cried

Martyn Layzell ©2002 Thankyou Music

Or thorns compose so rich a crown?
Were the whole realm of nature mine,
That were a offering far too small;
Love so amazing, so divine,
Demands my soul, my life, my all.

Isaac Watts, Lowell Mason, Public Domain

18. Jesus, all for Jesus
All I am and have and ever hope to be

For it's only in Your will that I am free
For it's only in Your will that I am free
Jesus all for Jesus
All I am and have and ever hope to be

All of my ambitions hopes and plans
I surrender these into Your hands

Robin Mark & Jennifer Atkinson ©1991 Springtide/Word Music

19. We sit here at Your feet
Where else could we go
To hear the Master speak words
That feed the soul?
Grace and favour, wisdom and truth
Are on the Master's lips
Ready to eclipse ungodly thought
Grace and favour, wisdom and truth
Timeless words of life
Timeless words of life

We look up to Your face
With open ready hearts
To hear the Shepherd's voice
Shed light upon our path

17. When I survey the wondrous cross
On which the Prince of glory died,
My richest gain I count but loss,
And pour contempt on all my pride.

Forbid it, Lord, that I should boast,
Save in the death of Christ, my God;
All the vain things that charm me most,
I sacrifice them to His blood.

See, from His head, His hands, His feet,
Sorrow and love flow mingled down;
Did e'er such love and sorrow meet,

Love and mercy, purity and peace
Are in the Shepherd's face
So, turning, we retrace our wayward steps
Love and mercy, purity and peace
Timeless words of life
Timeless words of life

So, give us ears to hear
The still small voice of calm
The subtle and the clear
The warning and the balm
Word of Jesus piercing like a sword
In the Master's hand
Helping us to stand and overcome
Word of Jesus, piercing like a sword
Timeless Word of life
Timeless Word of life

Grace and favour, wisdom and truth
Love and mercy, purity and peace
Word of Jesus, piercing like a sword
Timeless Word of life
Timeless Word of life

Philip Lawson Johnston ©1997 Kingsway's Thankyou Music

20. God in my living,
There in my breathing
God in my waking, God in my sleeping
God in my resting, there in my working
God in my thinking, God in my speaking
Be my everything

God in my hoping, there in my dreaming
God in my watching, God in my waiting
God in my laughing, there in my weeping
God in my hurting, God in my healing
Be my everything

Christ in me, Christ in me
Christ in me the hope of glory
You are everything
Christ in me, Christ in me
Christ in me the hope of Glory
Be my everything

Tim Hughes © 2005 Thankyou Music

21. I'm waiting for
The coming of my Lord
I'm waiting for the coming of my King
I'm longing for my Bridegroom to return
And I will watch, and I will watch
And I will cry with all my heart

Maranatha! Come, Lord, come!
Maranatha! When will You return?
Maranatha! Come, Lord come
Beloved Bridegroom come

How long until I see the One I love?
How long until I rest within Your arms?
How long until this aching heart is stilled?
And I will watch, and I will watch
And I will cry with all my heart

My lamp is filled, the flame is burning bright
I've gathered oil to last me through the night
And now I wait until my Bridegroom comes
And I will watch, and I will watch
And I will cry with all my heart

Ruth Fazal © Tributary Music 2003